Social Selling

A Facebook Tactical Guide

ARCTOSMEDIA

Written by Clifford VanMeter
Chief Marketing Technologist
Arctos Media, Inc.

Edited By Caitlin VanMeter

Table of Contents

"Strategy without tactics is the slowest route to victory. Tactics without strategy is the noise before defeat," Sun Tzu.

Introduction

It may surprise you to learn that your traditional marketing department is probably driving only about 30% of your total sales leads, and that's at their best. To be successful, you need to have your own lead-generation solution. The traditional process of sales prospecting and cold calling are long and tedious, producing limited results and making it hard to efficiently find high-quality sales leads.

Social selling is about leveraging your social network to find the right prospects, build trusted relationships, and achieve the sales results you need.

This sales technique enables a better sales lead generation and sales prospecting process and eliminates the need for cold calling. Building and maintaining relationships is easier within a network that you and your customer trust. Based on my experience, that network should primarily be Facebook, although these techniques can easily fit with profiles on other sites, like Twitter, LinkedIn, Pinterest, and more.

In the past, marketing was achieved by brute force, with broad and forceful tactics. I equate it to fishing with a net: We throw the net (advertising) out and hope to pull some fish back into the boat.

Social selling is more like spearfishing: one relationship at a time. Social selling has four pillars:

1. ***Build personal brand.*** Today's buyers have more opportunities and are more educated than ever. Information about you, the company you work for, and how you stack up against the competition is available at the click of a mouse. As a sales professional you serve two brands: your company and yourself. Building a strong personal brand requires you to be an active participant on social media. Doing so will lead to more engagement with your posts and make prospects more receptive to your communications.

2. ***Target the right prospects.*** Social selling enables you to find and connect with hundreds or even thousands of qualified

prospects much more effectively than traditional sales techniques. Recent studies have shown that more than 76% of potential buyers are comfortable discussing their needs on social media.

3. ***Engage with insights.*** Position yourself as an authority or expert by sharing relevant posts, commenting on the posts of others, and building your personal brand.

4. ***Build trust.*** Build trust with prospects by sharing your personal insights and helping provide relevant information. Be seen as a human being, rather than a selling machine, and have genuine conversations that focus on the needs of the prospect first, selling second.

One last note, although these techniques were hardened in the crucible of a Buy-Here-Pay-Here auto dealership, and I often use auto dealers as an example, these techniques can be used for any selling operation.

From dishwashers to doorknobs; from websites to wedding gowns; social selling is a clear and compelling sales tool that every salesman should have in their war chest. Done correctly, it's a boon to your success. Done improperly, it will quickly make you a pariah online.

Understanding The Customer

Before you begin social selling, really before you begin any marketing or prospecting efforts at all, you need to understand your customer.

It is vitally important that the content, social media, and search teams of your marketing department or company work together. A customer profile, sometimes called a buyer persona, is a good place to start. Who are your customers and what do they want?

Who are your customers?

It may be that the last time you read up on demographics was in school, and most of us didn't understand it then, either. These are the numbers and percentages that make up an audience description. What does the population look like? What ethnicities do they represent? What language do they speak?

For example, the demographic for Saturday morning cartoons is going to be kids, obviously, but different cartoons may narrow it down further by aiming at bilingual children, children of a specific age range, or even producing content specifically for girls or boys.

Your company probably already has a customer profile. If not they certainly should. You can easily pull the data together yourself to make a simple profile. This will at least get you targeting the right places.

Start thinking of demographics in a whole new light: how they relate specifically to your customer. On the next page you'll find a list demographic questions you should be able to answer about your customer. Knowing things like these about your customer may seem the most basic, but starting with a strong foundation when building a customer profile is important.

Building Your Customer Profile:

Use this worksheet to build a simple profile and get a handle on your demographics.

- What is my customer's age or age range? _____
- What is my customer's gender? _____
- What is my customer's relationship status? (Single, married, engaged?) _____
- Do they have or want to have children? _____
- What level of education do they have? (In school, High School Diplomas, or College?) _____
- What language(s) does my customer speak? _____
- What income range is my customer in? _____
- Where does my customer live? _____
- Do they live here 100% of the time or is travel involved? _____

These questions are going to need to be answered before you start asking yourself more probing questions.

What are their behaviors?

You need to know how your customers distribute their income and how they live their lives. The choices they make in their everyday behavior will help you be more targeted in your approach. What are their pain points, the things that worry them? How can you help them find what they are looking for, and assuage their fears and concerns? You should be able to answer the following behavior questions about your customer:

- How does my customer spend the money they make?
- How does my customer search for the service I provide?
- What services similar to mine has my customer used in the past?
- What hasn't been working for them?
- What professional and personal goals does my customer have?

What is your customer's personality?

Marketers call the process of exploring customer personality psychographics, as opposed to demographics.

This is a key part of building a customer profile and it can be the most fun, especially if you have an active imagination.

Remember to be honest when answering personality profile questions; you want to make sure you're targeting the customer you have, not the one you wish you had. You'll hear me talk about this idealized customer again later. It's a trap that many salespeople fall into. Take care it doesn't swallow you, too.

On the next page you'll find a form outlining some of the basic personality questions you should be able to answer about your customer.

Building Your Customer Profile Pt. 2:

This worksheet can help you build your
personality profile.

- What are my customer's hobbies or
  interests?

  _____

  _____

- What are my customers values or
  beliefs?

  _____

  _____

- What things (physical or conceptual)
  are important to my customer?

  _____

  _____

- How would my customer describe
  themselves?

  _____

  _____

Find the places your customers are attracted to, whether a physical location or an online space where they gather.

- Where do they hang out?
- What do they read, both online and offline?
- What do they search for online?

Review the needs and benefits that make your customers purchase your product or service.

- Where do they begin their research?
- What is their problem or need?
- What are the benefits to finding a solution?
- Do they make purchases by impulse?
- Do they seek out referrals or look at reviews?

One Size Does Not Fit All

Companies and customers are complex and they don't always fit a single customer profile. When you look at the data you have available, look for signs that you need to create more than one customer profile. It's often necessary to create a minimum of two or three customer profiles to fit different situations you may face. For example, if you have multiple locations you might find that the customer profile is a little different for each. Ethnicity, income, and home ownership… all these things can be affected by only a slight change in geography. With one of my clients, two dealerships less than 30 minutes apart have completely different customer profiles. Rural blue-collar whites dominate one dealership's customer profile, the other is predominately urban African-Americans. Still a third dealership, less than an hour away has a much more significant Hispanic customer base.

That brings us to *voice*. Your voice is the way you speak to various customer profiles; you may have to adjust it to appeal to different customer profiles.

Remember to keep in mind the company's overall strategies for social media, search, and content when thinking about your customers and how to properly target them.

How to Learn More

Even when you think you're sure about the customer profile you've created, I suggest going to your customer directly and double-checking everything. Sites like Survey Monkey, or even Google Docs let you create in-depth surveys that you can easily roll out to customers where you have their email addresses.

Incentivize these surveys in some way; though cash works best, almost any offer you make will help give them a little nudge.

In the end, would your customer answer these profiling questions in the same way you would? If not, confirm the answers so you don't risk embarrassing yourself, or worse losing money.

It's important that you have a realistic perspective on the customer you have. It's far too easy to develop what I call the idealized customer view. This is the customer you'd like to have, as opposed to the one you actually do have.

When creating a survey be as objective and neutral as possible. It's very easy to fall into creating what are called, *Push Surveys*. The questions are constructed to get a desired result, rather than a true result. Political polls often use push techniques when asking things like, "If you knew that the Candidate was being investigated for corruption, would you be less likely to vote for him?"

Reach out to your current customers. Just a few questions will help you gain insights into what made them choose you. Conduct informal interviews and ask them questions like those found on the next page.

Basic Customer Survey

Just a few questions will help you gain
additional insights into what made them
choose you. Conduct informal interviews
and ask them:

- How did you originally hear about us?

  _____

  _____

- What made you interested in our
  products or services?

  _____

  _____

- Why did you decide to purchase from
  us?

  _____

  _____

- What benefit or advantage did we have
  that other competitors couldn't provide?

  _____

  _____

- Are you still satisfied with your decision
  to purchase with us?

  _____

  _____

Not only will these informal surveys allow you to get in tune with your customer persona, but also they will start the social process.

Letting your customers know that you care about why they are your customers. It will instill the idea early on that you value their opinion.

It's a beneficial partnership, helping you to build a relationship with your customers for repeat business while allowing you to continually adjust your approach to attract new customers.

What is social selling?

Building a large following may initially appear to be the goal for social media, but there's no point in having a million followers if no one is buying. To get the most out of your social media it's less important to just be seen than it is to encourage action. On the other hand, shoving sales messages down people's throats will not encourage them to stick around.

While you may already be using social media to get your company name, products, and services out there, the buzzword of the moment is *social selling*, which is a far more tactical and integrated approach.

Social selling is about generating revenue and putting strategies in place that are designed to make a sale. From a conversion point of view it needs to lead to the product, not come from the product. Begin by thinking through your sales process from start to finish.

You are probably aware of the three-stage sales funnel. It's been around for years and it basically breaks down to what we show on the page following.

Browsers

People looking, but who have not yet decided to buy. They lack decisiveness.

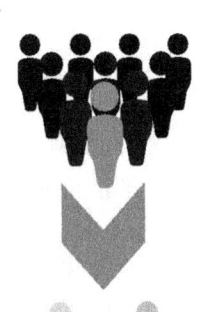

Lookers

Potential customers who have made the decision to buy, but have not yet decided when or where. They lack urgency.

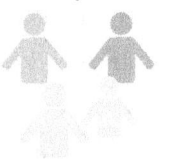

Buyers

These are the low-hanging fruit. Those people who have made a decision to buy and are looking to buy now. They only lack a compelling reason to buy from you, rather than your competitor.

Facebook is an amazing tool to push or pull prospects from one level to the next through the sales funnel.

Two things, the pursuit of pleasure and the avoidance of pain motivate people. Of those two, avoiding pain is by far the greater motivator, and it often motivates us to do nothing.

For example, the vast majority of people will tell you they aren't in the market for a new vehicle, but I am convinced that somewhere in the back of their mind everyone is looking for a nicer, newer ride. There will come a point when the pain of continuing to keep that old car outweighs the pain of spending the money.

That's the point at which they will need you, and if you've planted the seed and nurtured it properly, they will call you.

Social Selling Starter Tips

Potential Prospects

Worldwide, there are over 1.59 billion Facebook users active monthly. That's thousands or millions of potential customers out there, even on a local or regional level, just waiting for you to find them. One of the best things about Facebook is that it has opened up incredible possibilities for you to not only find these customers, but to target and connect with them.

> ## Remember This:
>
> **Facebook also operates in real-time, so you're right there at the right time to take full advantage of the needs of the prospective customer.**

Facebook has made it easier than ever before to research and pull together data that can help you tailor an approach to new customers, but with that great power comes great responsibility. You need to think about whom your target customer is and make sure you are listening to them. They're telling you what their needs are, what their pain is. Use that information to create an offer or a product that will take that pain away. That is the basis of all good sales: identify a need and offer a solution.

Remember, social selling is about creating relationships, which requires you to listen as well as speak.

Creating Credibility

You may have heard the adage, *"It's all about sincerity.... If you can fake that, you've got it made."*

Seriously though, generating and sharing interesting, and insightful content is a key part of social selling. This includes content that isn't seen as selling.

Things like recipes or funny videos can help establish your personal brand by creating a feeling of niceness about you. Your understanding of the customer has a direct impact on your credibility. Positioning yourself as an expert, sharing expertise, and giving a good impression across profiles, pages, and groups is critical to building trust. Training and experience play a critical part in creating your online personas and connecting with your prospects and customers.

Your Competition

Don't forget, social media can also help you track the competition. You should always be monitoring your competitors' pages to see what is and isn't working for them.

This will help inform your own content. How often do they post? How many likes do they have and how quickly they are adding new likes? Follow competitors and their employees to keep tabs on what they're talking about. You'll be surprised what you can pick up on.

Competition is good.

Social Selling Stats

Looking at social selling from the customer perspective, we see the following statistics that come into play. Obviously the customer perspective is often the most telling way to look at statistics.

- 79% of buyers said they used social media to research their buying decision before purchasing;
- 79% of salespeople who use social selling outsell their peers;
- 53% of buyers say they use social signals such as reviews and recommendations in making their buying decision. Up from just 19% in 2012;
- 54% of salespeople say they have closed one or more deals as a direct result of using social media;
- 93% of salespeople have received no formal training in social selling.
- 65% of buyers said the salesperson's profile or content had an impact on their buying decision;
- 84% of buyers viewed between five and eight pieces of content before contacting the salesperson;
- 64% of salespeople that used social selling hit their goal, compared to 49% who didn't use social selling.

Now here are some statistics from the point-of-view of your co-workers on the sales team.

These are statistics that affecting your personal performance right now, and every day. Be careful that you don't fall into one of these buckets.

- 93% of salespeople have received no formal training in social selling;
- 45% of salespeople who don't use social media say it's because they do not understand social selling;
- 53% of salespeople want help in understanding social selling.

Not only are these significant numbers, but also the increases across the board in just the last few years have been astounding. If you find yourself in one of these groups, those who don't understand how to best use social selling and/or those who want help, then this book is for you.

Facebook in a Nutshell

So now it's time to get to the meat of the matter: Facebook tactics that will generate leads that can translate into sales for you. I'll start with some basics on how Facebook operates.

It's important to understand the difference between a profile and a page: Profiles are for individuals and pages are for businesses. A profile can have up to 5,000 *friends*, while a page has no limit.

Once you have a profile, you can create a page; however, I recommend that you use the following prospecting techniques on your personal profile, not a business page. If you're only selling from your "Brand" (that is, from your Facebook page) you're missing out on practically unlimited possibilities to connect with prospective customers.

Social media is about people. Selling, especially social selling, is about developing relationships with prospects and converting them to customers. That's where Facebook starts to make sense — it's just another avenue (and a very important one in today's social media environment) to establish and grow personal relationships. If you have any lingering thoughts that using Facebook isn't worth the effort, consider the fact that 79% of salesmen who use social media as a selling tool get better results than those who don't.

Profiles

Before you begin prospecting on Facebook, you need to take stock of your Facebook profile. If you don't have a profile, that's fine, it takes just a few minutes to create one. If you already have a profile, skip to the next section "Optimizing an Existing Profile." Here's a brief step by step to setting up your profile.

1. Under the words "Sign Up" on the Facebook homepage, put your first name in the first box and your last name in the second box.

2. Next enter a valid email address and re-enter that email in the box below. This is so that Facebook can contact you for confirmation of your registration and in future sends you updates from your profile.

3. Enter a password of your choice, your sex, and your birthday. Then hit the Sign Up.

4. Facebook will send a confirmation email to your email account. In your email program, open the confirmation email from Facebook, and click on the link it provides.

Congratulations, you've just created a bare bones Facebook profile! Now, of course, hilarity will ensue.

Professional vs. Personal Profiles

Many people aren't comfortable using their personal profile as a prospecting tool. This is understandable; your personal and family connections may not be the same as your work connections. You don't say the same things in front of your prospects that you do to your poker buddies, for example. In addition, some people are reluctant to give customers access to that much personal information about them. Here's my recommendation: *Get over it.*

The only reason you might have for creating two separate profiles is if you say or show things on your personal profile that you wouldn't want your mother to see or hear.

Your profile makes you human. It shows who you are. Prospects will respond to that. Most will respond positively, a few negatively, but that shouldn't deter you from being yourself.

For the same reason, I would never create a dedicated page for prospecting (meaning a personal brand page, not a brand page for your company). Doing so basically conveys the message, "I'm a brand, not a person," to customers and prospective customers. People are less guarded when dealing with humans rather than companies. You'll have an easier time reaching out to people if you don't appear to be selling all the time.

Finally, if you create a page just for selling, you probably won't maintain it. Oh, you think you will, but if you have two social media profiles to update, eventually one will suffer. That will almost always be the second one.

Profile Recommendations

So the truth is that's not all there is to it. There are a few more steps to take to create a proper profile.

Technically, these aren't required, but I definitely recommend them. Here they are:

1. Personalize your profile by adding friends. Facebook will offer to scour your email address book for people with Facebook profiles, giving you a chance to add them as your friends. You can also choose people from your address book who aren't on Facebook and send them Facebook invitations.

2. Click the *Find My Classmates* button. Choose the country, city, name of your school, and the class year, and then click Search to find people you went to school with.

3. Click *Search For Your Co-Workers*, enter the company name and/or the name of the employee, and then click Search For Your Co-Workers to see what Facebook digs up.

4. The Facebook setup page offers the option to enter a city or town. Enter your city and click *Join*. Joining a regional network is useful because people within the same network can see more of each other's profiles even if they aren't friends.

So you may now by saying, "Why worry about my friends, coworkers and classmates? These aren't necessarily my customers or prospects." Well, there are two reasons:

1. A Facebook profile with no friends on it doesn't encourage people to accept your friend requests. This is the same reason they always leave a few coins in the wishing well. An empty wishing well doesn't encourage people to drop coins. Same for an empty Facebook page. I have 5,000 friends (the maximum number you can have on a profile). It took me about a year to break 1000, but only about another year to hit 5,000. Friends invite friending. So, yes. It does take time

to build your following, doing it the right way. Always bear in mind, *slow is steady and steady is fast.*

2. The average person on Facebook has about 300 friends. When you add a person to your friends list, they are basically giving you permission to talk to them. And you are also getting permission through them to talk to their 300 friends.

Optimizing an Existing Profile

Once you have a profile, it's time to take stock of it and see how you can use it as a channel to connect with customers.

My general rule of thumb is to make sure nothing there is overtly offensive. Although it may sound like a contradiction, be yourself, but don't necessarily be all of yourself. Remember that you're in a public forum and that the basic rules of public and workplace etiquette apply. Don't be a jerk. Don't belittle or demean others. Don't be racist, don't be nasty, and don't be mean spirited. Don't be a jerk (I said it already, but it bears repeating).

Do share the sort of things everybody shares, like pictures of your kids or your lunch. Talk about a thing you are passionate about, whether that's knitting, cars, hunting, computers, games, or food. In short, be a person. Be normal. Be approachable.

Also, as I mentioned above, make sure that all the fields in My Profile are filled in so you're sure that you're contactable. You can always change your privacy settings later on to adjust your experience.

Also, if your profile is still fairly new or empty, take a look at my previous profile recommendations to beef up your friends list and narrow down your profile details with your location and interests.

Facebook Visuals

The least you can do is add a profile picture, since it's the most basic identifier of you on Facebook.

Your profile pic appears in multiple places:

- Your friends' news feeds;
- Posts on your page's Timeline;
- Replies in comments;
- Comments and posts you make on other pages;
- And the cover photo on your Timeline.

The most important of these is the first one: the news feed of your followers. That tiny little icon that appears on others' feeds should be a recognizable personal branding tool. So be sure to choose a profile picture that works at all sizes, not just at the top of your profile.

To add a profile picture click the Picture tab to upload a picture from your hard drive. Click Browse, find a picture on your hard drive, tick the box to certify that you own the rights to the image, then click Upload Picture to confirm. Profile pictures are square and display at 160x160 pixels on your profile page. The photo you upload must be at least 180x180 pixels.

Here are my tips for creating a great profile pic:

- Use your logo if you have one.
- Minimize or eliminate all text

- If you're a business or brand, don't use a headshot (unless it doubles as your logo)
- Don't change it very often—consistency is the name of the game.
- Use an image that is recognizable on all social platforms
- Never use stock photos
- Make sure it's a square image

Your Facebook cover image is also important. It's the largest piece of real estate available for you to make an impression. This is the place where you have a lot more latitude to play, for example, making seasonal changes, displaying special offers, showing your brick-and-mortar locations, and so on.

According to a recent Forbes.com article, people decide in approximately seven seconds whether or not to trust you with their interests, so your cover image can carry a lot of weight.

Fortunately, choosing a great cover photo is not that tricky.

1. *Use the right image.* The best images will speak to your audience on an emotional level. You want to show

something that piques their interest and encourages them to learn more. The image should leverage your message and should be attractive, not just in the sense of being pretty, but also in the magnetic sense; it should attract viewers to you, your company, and your offering. For the optimal result the image needs to be sized to 851x315 pixels.

2. *Include a call to action.* Be judicious in adding text; I think less can be more in this case, so keep text on your cover photo to a minimum, although this doesn't mean you can't take full advantage of the possibilities. Facebook has historically been picky about the amount of text in cover photos, so keeping it minimal may help prevent problems if guidelines change down the line.

3. *Be promotional.* Many salespeople don't take advantage of the ability to change the cover photo as often as you like to display a variety of calls to action and themes. Is there a holiday coming up? Use that as a theme. Is your company running a contest? Mention it in the cover photo. This is your first impression, your best chance to present whatever you are pushing and promoting at that time.

Design Tips & Tools

As you probably know from sitting through sales or marketing PowerPoint presentations, design skills are not a prerequisite for being a good salesperson. If you're among the design challenged, you may be wondering how you're supposed to make your Facebook profile attractive.

Picasso once said, "All artists borrow, great artists steal." This means that a great artist can take the gist of what someone else has done and make it uniquely their own.

You don't have to be a great artist, or even a passable designer. There are millions of points of inspiration out there. See what your successful competitors are doing, then personalize a similar theme.

There are also a couple of great online tools that you can use that will help you create artistic memes, and cover photos.

My two favorites are:

Canva — This is an online design tool that makes creating cover photos as simple as answering multiple-choice questions.

- Start by signing up using Facebook.
- Next choose Facebook Cover Photo from the template bar at the top.
- You'll see a selection of templates running down the left side of the page, choose one you like and start modifying it.

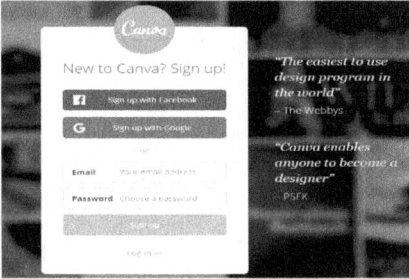

It's that easy. You'll end up with something professional and appealing in just a few clicks. Many of the images are free, a few cost $1 each, so you should be aware that it might cost you a buck or two by the time you're done.

Quozio — Visual quotes are inspirational quotes that include

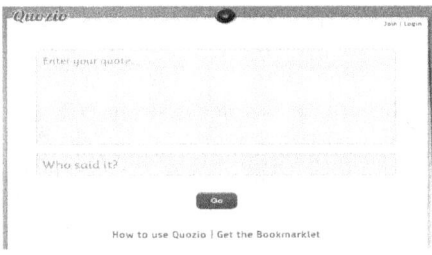

imagery. These are extremely popular content. Quozio provides you with a quick and easy way to make these visual quotes and memes. You can use the website and copy and paste a quote, or install the Chrome plugin so you can just highlight text on a page and hit create quote.

Engagement

Your Facebook posts support your Facebook prospecting efforts. The key is to generate engagement rather than to just post for the sake of posting. The three types of engagement, in order of importance are:

1. **Shares**. When someone (usually a fan) shares your post to all their friends. The average Facebook user now has about 338 friends. While not everyone on their friends feed will see everything of yours they share, the more the merrier.
2. **Comments**. Comments are an opportunity to interact directly with customers and prospects, Both you and your fans can comment on page posts, and on boosted posts (more on that later). This is where conversation marketing happens. It's true one-on-one engagement.
3. **Post Likes**. In the same way they can like your page, visitor can like a specific post. Post likes are good, but they aren't as important as comments or shares in communicating your message.

Private messages are another way of conversing with a customer or prospect. You can send a private message from your profile on the Facebook website, or through the messenger app.

Remember This:

It's important to monitor your profile for messages. Think of it like Facebook voicemail. This is where many, many of your customers will go to send support-related requests. They are asking for your help, so responsiveness is of the utmost importance, even if the response is just, "Call me, or PM me."

How to Stay Out of The Other Folder

It's also critical to understand the importance of the Other folder. The Other folder is where your messages go (other than friend requests) when you message someone who isn't on your already on your friend list.

It's also where messages to your profile (not page) will go when people who aren't friends try to message you. Most people don't ever check that folder, so they'll never know you tried to connect with them.

According to one survey, 40% of people don't even know they have an Other folder.

Below and on the next page you'll find some ways to avoid having your message go into the Other folder.

- Look for friends or customers that you've connected with using the Find & Friend method (which I'll detail a bit later) who have lots of friends. Message anyone with a fan page that has the message feature turned on. Don't be shy, these are great people to reach out to; they're usually industry leaders who have started fan pages to help build their businesses.

- Some businesses still have personal pages on Facebook, which means that when you friend that business, everyone else who has done the same thing could be your friend as well. Friend the business, then search the friend list for high-quality prospects. In Groups, click on the "People who like this" link; a pop up window will display those people. Hover over a name and then on the right you can add them.

- Through the messenger app on your phone you can even message people that are not friends of friends and it should still show up in their Inbox.

Warning: Don't do too many of these activities at once or Facebook might send you a warning or even shut down your account! Just do two to three per day. Use these techniques for just a few minutes every day and you'll be surprised at how much you can build your brand. At that pace, you could have 900 new friends in a year and the more friends you have, the easier it is to add.

A Great Facebook Message

Here's a good sample message, based on that format:

> *Hi, my name is Cliff. I'd been looking at your profile because I really enjoy the recipes you post. I saw your status update about your ongoing vehicle problems. I work for a local auto dealer, and I believe I can help. Message me back for details.*

As you can see, this message isn't pushy or spammy. Messaging people directly on Facebook must be subtle. The "I believe I can help," and "I know how you feel" messages are the two most effective because they show empathy.

More About Engagement

Your news feed displays the most relevant and important items on your profile. Using other people's posts as curated content is a simple process.

Your goal should be to both react to and get your posts shared and featured on your fans' news feeds.

Remember, the average Facebook user has nearly 350 friends. Those shares and comments go into the friend's newsfeed and straight out to their friends. So one share isn't one share, it's over 300 potential shares.

Sourcing Your Posts

Two of the best and easiest ways to generate topical and engaging posts are through content curation and content syndication. Along with content creation, these are the three components of content marketing, a buzzword you probably have heard if you've been involved in sales and marketing over the last couple of years.

Content curation is a method of pulling links, videos, and other content from your own profile and other sources. Content syndication is what you do with that material. These techniques are huge time savers in working social media effectively. They'll help you be active in the social media communities where your customers and prospects already are.

Success depends on knowing where your customers spend their time, knowing how to target them and how to engage with them. Engagement is the key to social selling. If you aren't giving them something of value, they will have no interest in staying engaged with you. They'll either become zombie friends (friends that lurk, but never comment, share or like) or they'll un-friend you.

Conversation marketing makes getting them to engage much easier and less time consuming. In addition to Facebook, other sites that provide both content for syndicating and venues for your syndication efforts include Twitter, LinkedIn, Craigslist, YouTube, Google+, and your own blog. We'll see in the coming pages how you can repurpose content from all those sites to create engagement on Facebook.

The Power of Like

On the whole, social media is aimed at making and maintaining connections with customers and potential customers, but it's also about getting people to like you. Not just in the Facebook *Like* sense, but in the sense of getting to know you as a person. Social selling is personal selling. It's about developing rapport.

In Robert Cialdini's great book, Influence, he defines what he calls the six pillars of influence, which could just as easily be called the six pillars of sales and marketing.

- Reciprocity
- Scarcity
- Authority
- Liking
- Consistency
- Consensus

The single most important of these pillars is *Liking*. People do business with people they like; this has been true throughout the entire history of the human race.

How do you get someone to like you? It's really quite simple. Find something you have in common. For example: You're on the phone with a prospect and you hear a dog bark in the background. So you ask the prospect, "What kind of dog do you have? Really? My dog is a...." Right there you've established an area of commonality: you both have dogs. In just five seconds, you've started to build a connection.

Although each of the various social media platforms provides a different kind of connection, as far as I'm concerned, Facebook is your number one resource for social selling.

Facebook makes up nearly 80% of daily social interactions. This means that Facebook is the 800-pound gorilla of social marketing, a beast that can heft the bulk of your marketing plan and bear the weight long term.

Getting Results

Social selling is about making incremental gains. This is spearfishing, remember?

At each stage of the process, you need to be aware of your incremental result. Your desired end result is obviously to close a sale, but in order to reach that you must first reach several smaller goals. For example:

- **Posting:** You're looking for engagement (on your profile) or response (in a group).
- **Private Messenger**: Your incremental result should be to get a prospect to the phone.
- **On the Phone**: Your goal is to set an appointment or get them in the door.

Keep the short-term result in mind. It's easy to fall into the trap of trying to push it too far, but you're not going to close the deal and deliver the vehicle over the Internet. It takes patience and subtlety to use social selling correctly.

Prospecting by Posting

The first step in Facebook prospecting is to establish your social presence. You do this by providing your Facebook friends with something other than an endless stream of sales pitches. It's important that you become part of their community.

At the same time you need to recognize that social media can be a huge time suck, unless you put processes in place to automate and control your Facebook presence.

Here are a couple general rules I train salespeople to follow to make sure that they are not overspending resources on Facebook maintenance:

- *Use the 5/1 rule.* For every selling post in your profile or page, you should post four items that have nothing to do with your product. However, these can be targeted to ensure maximum shares if you look at your customers' profiles to identify their interests. Google PPC (pay per click), through Google Adwords, lets you use Google to identify the things that your prospects are searching for. For example, if they are interested in cooking, restaurants, or sports, post about those things.

- *Use the One-Two-Three method* Keep your time spent on Facebook to a minimum, but get maximum effect.

1. At least one fresh post each day. This can be curated or original content. A link, a video, a picture, etc. Something that wasn't there on your page or profile the day before.

2. At least two comments or shares on posts by other people. This helps you build community. Ideally find things that your customers are already interested in and talking about. Get involved in the conversation.

3. Try to *Like* at least three posts by other people.

If all that takes you more than 10-minutes a day, you're doing it wrong.

Helpful Apps, Sites, and Resources

There are even free sites out there to help you manage your system:

Save time managing your social media
Schedule, publish and analyze all your posts in one place

Buffer (http://bufferapp.com). Buffer and the Buffer Chrome Browser add-on let you queue content to be posted later to any Facebook page or Twitter account you manage. For example, if you find a bunch of content on Monday, you can schedule curated posts for the whole week. You can even select frequency. I use Buffer to schedule curated posts like photos, links, and videos twice a day, at 9 a.m. and 6 p.m. Then I fill in throughout the week with some created content.

Buffer has also rolled out an add-on called Pablo (as in Picasso) that makes creating picture quotes quick and easy. Just select the text you want to quote and select *Quote in Pablo*.

Pocket (https://getpocket.com/a/queue/). This free app can help you find interesting items to share. Put them in your Pocket queue to review later. Pocket also gives recommendations based on links you've already saved. When you have time, review the links or videos, then Buffer them for posting.

Like Buffer, Pocket also has a Chrome add-on, which makes saving things as easy as a single click.

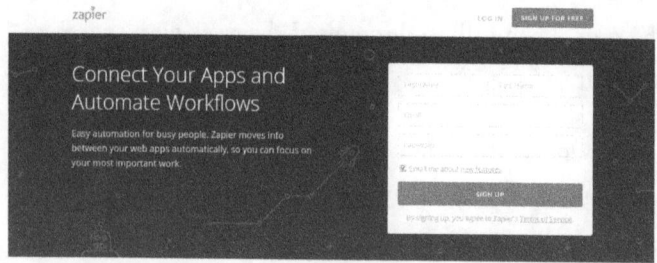

Zapier (https://zapier.com/). Zapier allows you to create Zaps, or "If/Then" links between web applications. You can create a Zap that automatically shares your blog posts or pushes new content from your YouTube channel to Facebook. The possibilities are endless and best of all, automatic. It takes a few minutes to create and test the Zaps, but once done you are on autopilot with your posting. Zapier guides you painlessly through the process of creating a new Zap. The most complicated thing s sorting through all the potential uses for Zapier; they provide recipes for commonly created Zaps.

Facebook itself also gives you some management tools for your posts. The Save for Later function lets you save videos or photos for later. Pull them up and Buffer them for distribution. You can also schedule posts for later right in Facebook.

The Dangers of Over-Automation

One of the goals of social selling is to present yourself as human. Too much automation will create a stream that has no human voice. Make sure that your automated posts are personal enough that your audience doesn't see you as a spam account. Finding the middle ground between automated posts and staying in the conversation is the key to success.

Remember This:

Once you have set up social media automation, you can't just forget about it. To have a successful account, you need to monitor your progress. You have to keep connected and engaged with your audience from the beginning to the end. From your first post to your last.

Understanding which parts of social media to automate can be a challenge. Remember the Rule of 5/1? Of every five items you post, only one should be sales oriented. For the four remaining, up to three can be content from someone else, but at least one should be your original content that is relevant, but not a sales pitch. At least two posts should be something personal, something that makes you seem more human and approachable.

One way to work the social media automation system, yet keep a human voice, is to automate posts that are not that important. Picture quotes (like I mentioned above) or memes can be automatically posted when you're out of the office. These kinds of posts will be equally relevant at any time and will continue to humanize your account. The real aim of automated posts is to maintain a presence. Posts like quotes and memes won't be seen as spam so long as you mix them up with personal and topic-related posts.

There are definitely times, however, when you shouldn't use automated posts, such as in dealing with customer relations. The way you respond to customers online can mean the difference between keeping and losing them. An impersonal automated response is going to put anyone off contacting you. People like to talk to other humans, not an automated robot.

A similar no-no is automating troubleshooting; if you do this via automated posts you will lose customers.

One way of working the social media automation system and keeping a 'human' voice, is to automate posts that are not that important.

Examples of this would be quotes, or memes. These can be automated at times of the day where you're away. These kinds of posts will make sense at any time and continue to humanize your account.

Really the aim of automated posts is to maintain a human presence. There I go, using that word human again, but that's just it… human is what you want to be. Be a person. To quote Oscar Wilde, "Be yourself, everybody else is already taken." Posts like quotes and memes aren't going to be seen as spam so long as you mix them up with personal and topic related posts.

There are definitely times when you shouldn't use automated posts. Such as when dealing with customer relations. The way you respond to customers online can mean the difference between keeping and losing a customer. An impersonal automated post is going to put anyone off contacting you. People like to be talked to by other humans not by an automated robot.

Another big no-no is automating troubleshooting. This is similar to customer responses and will have the same outcome if done via automated posts – you will lose customers.

Where? What? When?

So we've covered the where (Facebook) and the what (content), let's take a look at the "*When*".

Facebook's internal audits have shown that the best time to post for maximum engagement is between 13:00 and 16:00 (that is, 1 p.m through 4 p.m.) during the week, with Wednesday as the peak day.

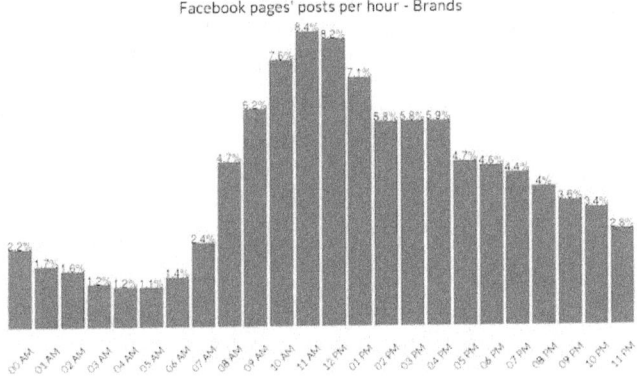

Facebook pages' posts per hour - Brands

As you can see from the graph above, weekends are bad for engagement overall, so you should avoid posting on Saturdays and Sundays. Also avoid posting before 8 a.m. and after 8 p.m., as these times show a sharp drop off in engagement.

The answer to *when* also brings up the question of how often. The answer is a simple one:

- Brands that post less than once per day get 40% less engagement than brands who do.
- Brands that post more than twice a day get 20% less engagement.

That's right, posting too much is as bad as not posting enough. So the answer is simple: twice a day in the afternoon.

If you want to set a more definitive schedule, try posting once on Mondays and Fridays, twice on Tuesdays through Thursdays, and lay off entirely on the weekends.

Building Your Facebook Audience

Facebook offers the best opportunity to connect directly with our customers and their connections. Remember the average Facebook user has more than 300 friends. When they give you permission to talk to them, they're also giving you permission to talk to their friends, albeit indirectly through their newsfeed.

Why is it important to connect with customers' connections? People tend to cluster in like-minded groups. These groups, which master marketer Seth Godin calls *Tribes*, tend to be homogenized along certain lines. So if your customers are there, the other members of the *tribe* are likely to be demographic, psychographic and even geographic look-a-likes to your customers.

In other words, we tend to connect with people, who are like us in some way. Economically, socially, or with similar hobbies and interests. So one of the best places to prospect for new contacts is going to be through your old contacts.

Here are four tactics that I've found work best for building your Facebook audience as quickly as possible:

- **Find and Friend.** Find your existing customers and prospects on Facebook, and send them a friend request. Then use some further prospecting techniques we'll explore later in this book to connect with their friends.

- **Post.** Post on your Facebook page regularly. As I've noted, and will continue to note, four out of five posts should be focused on things your customers are interested in, but not direct selling. About one out of five times you can post a direct call for leads, or a request for referrals.

- **Comment.** Comment on posts made by your customers. You probably shouldn't, for example, comment on the announcement of a new baby by pointing out that you have a large stock of minivans. On the other hand, if you want to donate a month's supply of diapers to the new family, Facebook might be a great place to make that announcement. Create good feelings with your comments.

- **Groups.** Groups are a great way to become active with a community, but targeting groups with promotions can be tricky. Group administrators don't appreciate what they see as spammy content. However, many groups give you the opportunity to post the equivalent of classified ads that will be seen by hundreds or even thousands of people. As with posting on your Facebook profile, only about 20% of your group posts should be direct selling. Be an active member of the group, commenting and posting non-sales related content. This helps to ensure you don't get banned.

Facebook's Search Field

The first place to start searching for prospects is, oddly enough, the Facebook search field. The most powerful search query, ISO, or in search of, provides a way to find people who are looking for products or solutions like those you offer: ISO used cars, ISO new car, ISO transmission repair.

That last one is especially great for BHPH dealers. Transmission repairs are costly; simply by contacting those people and offering them a viable alternative to a $2000-$3000 repair, you can find qualified and willing prospects.

That last one is one of my favorites, especially for BHPH dealers. Transmission repairs are costly. Simply by contacting those people and offering them a viable alternative to a $2000-$3000 repair, you can find qualified and willing prospects.

The Chrome Search Plugin

If you are not using the Chrome browser, you absolutely should be. It's the most advanced browser available, and offers the most sophisticated tools to help you manage web apps such as Facebook. There is a spectacularly useful Chrome add-on for Facebook searches that offers many more options than the basic Facebook search. To add it:

1. Click *More Tools* in the menu on the right of the screen;

2. Select *Extensions*, and at the bottom of the Extensions page;

3. Click *Get More Extensions*;

4. On the Chrome Web Store page, enter *Facebook Search* in the search field and;

5. Select Extensions from the radio buttons below the search field;

6. See the correct extension in the screenshot on the following page, with the ribbon (because I already have it installed).

Once you install the extension, it will show up on your address bar along with any other add-ons you have installed, as in in the graphic below:

Click the icon to launch the search menu.

This is when it gets interesting; the search functions give you so

many opportunities to create lists of potential prospects using the find & friend method.

The *AND* operator lets you

create multiple joined searches. For example, if you are located in Kalamazoo and a number of your current customers work for Wal-Mart, enter those terms into the *Lives Present* and *Job Present* fields to get a list of people who live in Kalamazoo proper and work for Wal-Mart.

One of the simplest and best places to start is the *Friends Of* search. Find a current customer and use this search to target their friends. Because people tend to flock like birds, the friends of a customer who you've friended are likely to be great prospects to target.

Here are a few other recipes you can use for more complex searches:

- If you know you have several customers who work for a local employer, combine Lives and Job to find people who work there and live in your area.
- Combine Lives and Job to find people who work for those common employers who live in other areas you haven't prospected before.
- Use Group Member to find people who belong to the groups you target.
- Use Like to find people who like your competitor's' pages. Try mixing and matching searches. Be careful not to get too

narrowly focused, though, or you'll end up filtering out all or most of your results.

- Use the Like field to find people that like competitors' pages. If these are direct competitors, you're virtually guaranteed to find a demographic match for your customers.

What do I mean by "direct competitors"? If you're a BHPH dealer and you're targeting the Ford dealership you won't get good results. They are not your customers. You need to be more directed, more targeted. Again, it's all about knowing who your customer is. If you know your target customer, you'll know who your competitors are. If they are targeting the same people as you they are your competitors.

Prospecting in Groups

Facebook has thousands of groups, on almost any topic you can imagine. They're based on shared. As I mentioned before, many of these groups give you the opportunity to post the equivalent of classified ads. Something as simple as:

> *Looking for a reliable used vehicle? Bad credit? I can help.*
> *PM me for details.*

You'll get responses; so pay attention to your messages and especially to your *Other* folder. Remember, when you receive a message from people who aren't on your friend list, that's where it goes.

 The key thing is to answer quickly and keep in mind the most important goal of PMing a prospect: to get them off PM and on to the phone as quickly as possible. The hard truth is that you're never going to close a sale on PM. In fact, if you're too free with information through Facebook Messenger you're discouraging a potential customer from calling or meeting with you in person.

Inertia is a powerful force. Inertia is a scientific term best described by Newton's first law of motion, which says, *"An object at rest tends to remain at rest. An object in motion tends to stay in motion."*

Cliff's first law of prospects is, *"A prospect on their couch tends to find reasons to stay on their couch. A prospect in your office tends to stay in your office."*

Give prospects a reason NOT to come in, and they'll take it every time. So giving them all the information they need via a message will do more harm than good. The short-term goal of the Facebook message is to move them to the phone, not to sell them a car or even to set an appointment.

You can do this with one simple phrase that we have found to be very effective.

I talk faster than I type, what's a good number to reach you?

Most people will give you that number. Once they do, ask them this:

And what would be a good time to call?

You've just generated a qualified lead. You have a name, a phone number, and a best time to call. The amazing thing about this lead is that when you call they will answer. This will increase your contact rate tremendously and that's an important KPI. We track that contact rate for our salespeople as a key indicator of how they are doing overall. It's simply the number of contacts made out of the total number of calls made (Contacts/Calls=Contact Rate). A low contact rate almost always indicates that they've fallen into the routine of always calling at the same time of day and need to randomize their calling schedule. It also indicates that they aren't using the techniques outlined in this book.

There is no quicker way to increase this percentage than by using Facebook to make the initial contact and set a time to call. Cold calling throughout the day, especially with ubiquitous Caller ID, just doesn't produce the results needed to maintain a high contact rate.

If you want to make more sales, the place to start is more contacts. Most companies don't actually need more leads; they need a better contact rate. The benchmark we use is 30%—30 out of every 100 calls should result in a contact, meaning an actual conversation with a human being, not a voicemail.

More contacts will lead to more appointments, which will lead to more sales. So, going back to the idea of a classified ad. What type of groups would be best to post in? Here again, knowing your customer and their interests is paramount. For example, garage sale groups are great for BHPH targeting but might not be right if you're a Lexus dealer. Think about your prospects' habits and the brands they follow. Is your customer more likely to be a Wal-Mart shopper or a Macy's shopper? Starbucks or McDonalds?

The other trick is whether you'll be allowed to post without getting shut down by the group admins. This requires some research and subtlety. It also requires some level of involvement beyond just showing up and throwing ads at people. One of the key things is being active in the group on a regular basis.

When searching for groups don't forget that computers are like a big box full of idiots; they only respond to exactly what you ask them. For example, one company where I was marketing manager had a primary location in Kalamazoo, but there were dozens of smaller communities, townships, and villages nearby.

Remember This:

Be careful not to get too narrowly focused with your searches. You'll end up filtering out all or most of your results and be left with nothing. Keep to two search terms at the most and if you add a third make sure it is related to one of your other two searches.

Searching for a group using the search term Kalamazoo Garage Sales didn't give me similar groups in those other areas. However, searching for Groups Like Kalamazoo Garage Sales in the Facebook search bar gave me a great list of other groups to target in surrounding areas. For an even more focused list, I could search for groups within a reasonable driving distance by entering the names of communities. For example, I could search for communities with populations over 2000, within 25 miles of Kalamazoo, MI.

Wikipedia is a great source for finding surrounding communities; search for the largest town or the county and you'll find a list of nearby communities.

You can take it further by cross-referencing that information with Census data, as I've done using Data USA (datausa.io).

Automated Posting

Many programs, add-ons, and extensions are available to help you automate posting to Facebook Groups, but I don't recommend this as a rule. The trick with posting to groups is not to overdo it and a high volume of cross posting is bad form.

Just as with your personal posts, you can automate some of the group posting, but the same caveats apply. If you use auto-posters to push spammy content out to groups on a regular basis you'll end up getting ejected from the group. Ideally, your posting frequency should be no more than once or twice a week. Other than that, you should be active in the group by liking, sharing, and commenting.

I've worked with salesmen who belong to as many as 80 groups, but I recommend no more than 15 to 20. That's a manageable number; it means that if you post to each group once a week, that's three or four posts per day during the week (remember, I don't advise posting on weekends). A couple of quick comments, a few likes, a sprinkling of posts, and you're done for the week for that group.

Again, group posting is only effective if you're seen as an active participant and you don't abuse it.

Facebook Messenger

Recently Facebook introduced several new features for Facebook Messenger that can be used to make contacting your brand easier. These include Usernames, Links and Messenger Codes. The best thing about these new features, in my opinion, is that phone numbers aren't necessary, and you don't have to be friends on Facebook.

These new features are going to allow your customers and prospects to start conversations immediately. Messenger Codes are one of the easiest ways to find people and be found in Messenger.

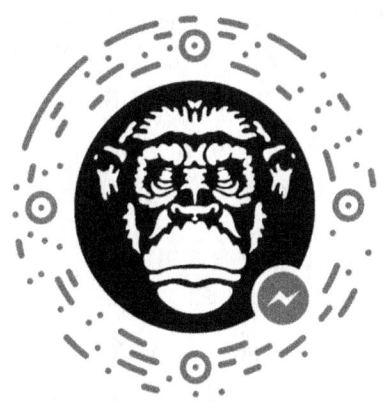

It doesn't matter if you are standing next to them, or on the other side of the world looking at your computer screen. No matter where you are all you have to do is share the scan-able code with your audience and they can connect to you in a couple of clicks. No more back and forth with texts trying to make sure you have the right number saved and awkwardly asking people how to spell their names. Your settings tab in Messenger has your Messenger Code displayed prominently.

Sharing can be done online, in emails, or in print. Try adding your Messenger Code to the back of your business cards, or to your flyers and other ads; even on in-store posters. How about adding them next to your buyer's guides, or on rack cards and other marketing materials? Of course you'll certainly want to add them to your web pages.

Messenger Links and Usernames are another type of link that you can share from your email signature or your website. You can send your Messenger Link directly to your contacts or friends. Tap or click any Messenger Link to open Messenger directly to a thread with that person or business when using a mobile device. You can find and share your username from your Settings tab.

Of course using messenger provides you with one more contact pipeline for your customers. Phone, text, messages, Facebook comments; these are all just open conduits to start the conversation. The more you have, the easier it becomes for your customers and prospects to connect with you.

Responding to Comments

Be prepared to get comments, both on your profile posts and in groups you frequent. There are four ways to react to comments or reviews: ignore, acknowledge, respond, or ban/report.

One of the biggest reasons people ignore online comments and reviews is that they dread responding to them.

They are simply reluctant to get involved with a customer in a public forum; they see it as setting a dangerous precedent. Give in to one customer, and suddenly everyone will be on Facebook every time they want to score some free upgrade.

> ## Remember This:
> Companies start out guilty on the Internet. It's important that you take the time to respond to public criticism publicly and reasonably. That means no personal attacks, no blaming the victim (even if they aren't really the victim), and no getting angry.

Just as often, you simply don't know what to say, and don't want to say the wrong thing. The truth is, the wrong thing to say is nothing. Under every circumstance, failure to comment or reply is seen as an admission of guilt.

Even if their post is untrue, it's important to remain calm and be SEEN to be the reasonable one. This is how you reverse the, "...companies are always wrong," perception. Once you become the reasonable one, other Facebook users and your customers will turn on the original poster. Let them get angry for you. Let them say the things that you desperately want to, but can't. Well shouldn't, anyway.

Here are a few tips on how to respond:

- **Respond quickly and accurately**.
- **Show gratitude and respect**. Never, ever respond in a negative or offensive way.
- **Include facts and data, not opinions.** If it's possible to link to factual data, do so, but don't expose personal information about the commenter.
- **Respond in a tone of voice that reflects the company's values and culture**.

- **Be transparent**. Let the commenter know how you're connected with the company. Never pretend to be a customer, if you aren't. In fact never pretend to be anything or anyone you are not.

It's also important to look at your company's social media policy. If it doesn't have one, I suggest putting one in place immediately. Assign a single person to monitor comments and reviews and give that person the responsibility and authority to respond. If this isn't practical, a more involved solution is to give everyone the authority and training to speak to reviews and comments.

I believe this is the best solution, though obviously training becomes an integral aspect of the way people will respond.

Your settings are also important. I recommend that you start by changing two key settings:

1. **Change Visitor Postings.** It should be set to, "Review posts by other people before they are published to the page."

2. **Set the Profanity Filter to Strong.** This will automatically kill many troll-ish comments, since these often include profanity. With this setting at it's highest, even mild profanity will be blocked. While the troll will still see his or her comment, no one else will.

You've probably heard the maxim, "Don't feed the trolls." Trolls are online commenters who speak broadly, without specifics and often in the most offensive ways possible, posting comments like, "I hate these people," or, "XYZ Company sucks."

I'm of the opinion, though, that you should sometimes feed the trolls' detractors, people I call the troll hunters. Troll hunters are just waiting to take a bite out of the first troll who comes along. While the times to break out the troll bait are few, when one actually has something to say, you can respond as shown below. Let's look at the most common scenarios in turn:

- **Positive & False:** Thank them for their comments, but don't correct the misinformation unless it is directly tied to your presence, such as hours or location.
- **Positive & True:** Thank them for their comments.

- **Negative & Troll:** "You suck," doesn't exactly give you a lot of room for engagement. Trollish comments like this should be deleted and the troll banned. For reviews, if there is any use of profanity or any other violation of Facebook rules you can report it. Otherwise, since you can't delete Reviews, ignore those kind of reviews. No good with come from engaging on this. There is nothing to engage on.

- **Negative & Not a Troll & Erroneous/Untrue:** Correct the misinformation as politely and directly as possible.

- **Negative & Not a Troll & True**: This is where a sincere, "I'm sorry," carries a lot of weight. Add a, "Please contact me directly so I can try to resolve the issue and re-earn your trust." Simple and direct.

- **Negative & Troll & True**: This is the time to whip out the troll bait. Engage the troll and try to change either the perception of the situation or their opinion. Often these comments will end up being the, "I heard from a friend of a friend", variety. Once you reveal that fact, people lose confidence in what the troll has to say, or they'll simply stop responding themselves. This is exactly where the troll hunters come in as well. Good customers will reply to the negative comments, and often in ways that you as a representative of the company cannot.

Create Benchmarks

The volume of negative feedback you receive is influenced by a number of factors including how much reach you get, the size and quality of your audience, and the specific industry.

All these factors are unique for your company, so there is no way I can tell you specifically the number of negative comments that are acceptable. Many marketers would say *none*, but I'm a bit more realistic.

I suggest you work with your marketing department and general managers to determine what an acceptable level of negative feedback would be and establish benchmarks based on the average volume of negative feedback you receive.

You should then set goals for decreasing your negative feedback average to help maximize your post reach. Be particularly aware of the times when your marketing staff is boosting a post. Boosted posts re going to get increased the level of comments, and you want to encourage that. Remember comments are one of the best ways to get more exposure through engagement.

Once you've established a realistic baseline for negative comments and reviews, you should do all you can to help marketing keep the volume below the baseline. The way to do this is simple and requires very little effort on your part. Ask for the review at the time of sale and/or encourage your customers to write a positive reply to a negative review.

You'll be amazed how successful you'll be by doing that one thing, *asking.*

Online & Dealership Acronyms

Every industry has its own language. The online world is filled with acronyms. As much as I've tried to make this book relatively jargon-free, it's good to understand what these mean. You're sure to encounter most or all of these in the course of mastering online marketing.

SRP – Search Results Page: A dynamically created webpage that shows the vehicle results of a specific search query on a car dealer's website.

VRP – Vehicle Results Page: Same as SRP, depending on the company some may use VRP in place of SRP

VLP – Vehicle Listings Page: This is generally a listing of available inventory on the dealer's website. This will be distinct from VDPs because it will list a number of vehicles. Depending on the company some may use VLP in place of SRP.

VDP – Vehicle Details Page: A page on an automotive retail website that represents a single, specific vehicle. This is where a consumer finds all the information related to a vehicle.

UX – User Experience: A term that's meant to subjectively quantify what a consumer's experience might be using a website. A good UX is one that's easy to navigate, is mobile responsive and anticipates the consumers needs.

ADF – Auto-lead Data Format: An XML based standard for taking customer information submitted via a form on your or a 3rd party website and inputting it directly into your CRM.

BDC – Business Development Center: A department within a dealership that's tasked with driving and retaining traffic for the sales and/or service teams of the store. There are various ways to staff a BDC, but in general the personnel handle some or all of the inbound phone calls, Internet leads, unsold follow up & retention activities.

CRM – Customer Relationship Management: A CRM gives a dealership's sales team a way to track, manage and follow up with each customer that submits a lead, call the dealership and/or walks through the door.

DMS – Dealer Management System: A software system with modules withfor sales, finance, service, parts and administration. Vehicle inventory data feeds are also parsed through the DMS.

GA – Google Analytics: The free analytics suite that you'll find installed on the vast majority of car dealership websites.

PIT – Precise Interest Targeting. For Facebook this kind of precision targeting is accomplished using custom audiences and/or lookalike audiences. These audiences target a specific subset of Facebook users who are more likely to be receptive to your ad.

UV – Unique Visitors: Often simply *Users* within Google and other Analytics, this is the number of individual people who visit a website

BR – Bounce Rate: Expressed as a percentage, bounce rate is a function that occurs when a user navigates away from a website after viewing only one page.

TOS – Time on Site: Also known as Session Duration in Google Analytics, this is the average amount of time in minutes and seconds a user spends on a website in a single visit. More time on the site generally leads to higher conversions.

SERP – Search Engine Results Page: The list of results a search engine displays after a user enters a search query.

SEO – Search Engine Optimization: A set of strategies and tactics implemented on a website to gain visitors by achieving a higher organic ranking on search engine result pages.

SEM – Search Engine Marketing: The process of driving web traffic by purchasing text ads on search engines such as Google and Bing. SEM is often referred to in general as Paid Search.

CPC – Cost Per Click: The measurement of the cost per click for campaigns based on impressions.

PPC – Pay Per Click: The measurement of campaigns where you only pay if a user clicks. Paid search is the most relevant example of PPC – while your ad may show up in a SERP, you only pay your ad is clicked.

CTR – Click Through Rate: This measures the percentage of clicks per impressions an ad receives.

CPM – Cost Per Thousand: No that's not a typo; the M in CPM stands for mile, which is Latin for thousand. A common measurement used across digital and traditional advertising that refers to the price a network charges for one thousand ad impressions.

eCPM – Effective Cost Per Mile: This metric accounts for over or under delivery of an impressions based campaign. Campaigns that over delivered will give you an eCPM lower than the CPM you actually paid and a campaign that under delivers impressions will give you an eCPM higher than what you actually paid.

KPI – Key Performance Indicator: Is a metric or group of metrics a dealership will use to determine performance in specific areas of operations. You might have KPI's for your website, SEO, customer retention and so on.

ROI – Return on Investment: I would think everyone would know this one, but just incase…ROI is the profit earned from a specific advertising campaign.

GTM – Google Tag Manager: A free tool that makes it easy for marketers to setup and manage conversion tracking, site analytics, remarketing and other tags on your website.

SMM — Social Media Marketing: Basically what this book is about. Strategies and tactics to optimize your social media campaigns to deliver high conversions rates and great ROI.